Novelty Theory

by Caspar Heinemann

Published 2019 by The 87 Press LTD
87 Stonecot Hill
Sutton
Surrey
SM3 9HJ
United Kingdom
www.the87press.com

ISBN 978-1-9164774-3-8

Design: Stanislava Stoilova [www.sdesign.graphics]
Cover Image: 'Punk Rock Possibility' © Jake Kent 2018

Contents Page

HIGH AMBIGUATION SUMMER FEAST HOPING

ANOTHER WORLD IS POSSIBLE IT HAS TO
BE CRACKED OPEN ANYWHERE SOFT AND
MILITARY SURPLUS SEWN GETTING LUCID
STRUCTURAL GAVE ME HOPE SOMEHOW

SOMETHING NO MOVEMENT UNTIL THERE
IS A PLACE TO GO THAT IS NOT ALREADY
SUCKED SATURATED HOLDING HANDS WITH
EFFEMINATE LAMPPOSTS WHISPER SWEET

PRE-NOTHINGS ABOUT BEFORE THE FALL S
IT FEELS UTOPIAN WHICH IS AN IMPRECISE
MEASUREMENT OF THE WORLD FOSSILISED
OUTSIDE GENTRIFICATION IS A DEAD LANGU

PLANTED DEAD COPS ALONG THE ROADSIDE
SAVED THE RAINWATER FOR BETTER THINGS
COUNTED NIGHTS WEIGHTED EXPECTANTLY
IN THE GREATEST GREENHOUSES WE COULD

BUILD BETWEEN JOYLESSLY INTACT PLATE
GLASS DISGUSTS ME BETTER THAN ANYTHI
MOVIE THEATRE CRUISES HARDWARE STOR
WE NEED BOTH BEFORE DECOMPOSITION

JOYFUL FAITH FAG GROWING BETTER NEW
NEGATIONS FOR OLD PROBLEMS AGAIN TO
FEEL LIKE WHAT IS THERE TO BE NOW THAT
WE HAVE ALL THIS SPACE!!!!!!!!!!!!!!!!!!!!!!!!!!!!!!!!

KNITTING TEMPLES TO SOME GODDESSES
GOBLETS OF THE 1ST SUMMER BUCKFAST
GIVE PRAISE TO BUDDLEJA CANAL FIGHTS
RETURNING REWRAPPED GIFTS EARNEST

GRATITUDE IN EVERY LAVENDER BUSH SET
TO A SUCCESSION OF REPETITIVE BEATS !
GROWING NEW STEMS TO SHARE YR LAST
CIGARETTE WITH LAST FRIEND STANDING

FAITH BASED ARTIFICIAL LIMBS HOLDING
FEATURE LENGTH MAGICAL CIRCLE JERK
NOVELS IN SOFTWOOD TREE GOUGINGS
CARE CARVED W TIGHTENED LIMP WRISTS

NATURAL RESISTANCE TO OBJECTS OF
BOREDOM FUCKING DAISY CHAINS WITH
FRIENDS FOREVER AGAIN AND AGAIN LET
PEOPLE FIND THEIR OWN MUDBATHS OK

SOMEWHERE OVER THE LOW HANGING
BLOSSOM TREES SCRAPING HEADS OF
STATE SANCTIONED VIOLENCE FEELS AS
DISTANT AS NEVER BEFORE!!!!!!!!!!!!!!!!!!!!!!!!!!!

Untitled (A Farewell to Progress)

'If you are in a shipwreck and all the boats are gone, a piano top buoyant enough to keep you afloat that comes along makes a fortuitous life preserver. But this is not to say that the best way to design a life preserver is in the form of a piano top. I think that we are clinging to a great many piano tops in accepting yesterday's fortuitous contrivings as constituting the only means for solving a given problem.'

- Buckminster Fuller

'We're kids building models of a world that we might wanna live in / And sorting feelings in our stomachs - is this liberation or starvation? / But have we made it anywhere at all if the dishes are never done? / If we can't live without dishwashers, how could we live without cops?'

- Wingnut Dishwasher's Union

O Retro anarcho-primitivist critique of the magnificent rinsing
      rising centre that never actually existed but Eugene, Oregon,
1990-something still life with riot-grrl melts so cold
      ice cube in cheap white wine
is a lucky place to find redemption relatively folded
      because It is 2017 for now and I am listening to Cornelius
Cardew's 1974 work 'Revolution is the Main Trend'
because I am a very classy   Maoist
                        red wine breath on Guardian article on
Paradise papers
      field mice counting stars to be added to the census on distant
                                    fields of planetary rupture
2012 actually happened, that's how we use actually now, but
            it did actually happen
                  because i really meant *everything* entirely as usual
writing sonnets to exceeding the rubber touch of the Welfare State
                        for a towering seaweed Wicker Man here to
milk the blood moon for tidal bounty beach balls
                        Mayday
a fountain of obscure Marxist-Leninists glistens in the midday
sunset

                        and/or becomes incommensurable
immeasurable tanks between positions is a boring knife
                  to die under ACTION BEFORE WORDS OR

WHATEVER that EARTH FIRST! slogan was
beneath the No More Panic
Health Anxiety forum, the feral furry skin
the fact that nobody has ever spelt bureaucracy right first or even second time
1968 Decorative Memorial Plate that i hate
that i hate every coffee shop i have ever wrote a poem in because
they are the enemy and yet - another
delicately mortgaged microcosm of the problem
lukewarm cortado frothing at the mouth
smashed Starbucks window Seattle 1999 did they even smash
a Starbucks it doesn't matter
astute market forces not yet windblown to smithereens
The Anti-Globalisation Movement Aesthetic
left over left bubble mix
despite 1917 i am an avocado on the toast of late capitalism
this poem won't age well but politics should hope to age badly
and anyway
fortunately
time doesn't exist
FUCK CORPORATE PRIDE ~ STONEWALL WAS A RIOT ~
STONEWALL WAS A FUNERAL FOR JUDY GARLAND
AND IF THERE WERE MORE FUNERALS LIKE THAT
WE MIGHT BE GETTING SOMEWHERE
fire extinguisher thrown off the roof of
a building 2010 falling fire
extinguisher the most beautiful metaphor
FIRE EXISTS AND FIRE EXITS!
The Chicago Seven (originally Chicago Eight, also Conspiracy
Eight/Conspiracy Seven also Stoke Newington Eight
STEAL THIS PRAXIS
the more things stay the same the more they change the
same 1969 happens forever
neon pink soldiers killing everything right now again
paw prints across the pentagon across or against
Stoke Newington Police Station burnt down again to its natural
state of restfulness
watching burning sensations as they arise in the body
is the main thing to do in these days of water beds / need
instruments
August 1970 to August 1971
in the swampy remains of culture soggy burnt rice in
the eyes culture i.e. the island

i am from in this life of elastic and springy bread dough
the future frames a guilty man
Stop the City and Reclaim the Streets and a line of dates and a
line of riot cops
despite the failings of the movement to move
when was glass invented when were bricks invented when was tactical smashing invented?
a brick through a window as if for the very first time
did Benjamin invent glass? did the Luddites invent total destroy?
Once I had a love and it was a gas
Soon turned out had a heart of glass
Seemed like the real thing, only to find
Mucho mistrust, love's gone behind
Lost inside
Adorable illusion and I cannot hide
I'm the one you're using, please don't push me aside
fight gentrification ~ be our own PR managers
and bring back the kombucha health scare
'situationism' or as i like to call it a marker pen smiley face
on the traffic lights of history
LONDON. ACID. CITY. LONDON. ACID. CITY.
no offence BUT the past 10,000 years
begin quote 'Song of the Workers' of the 1848 Revolution' end quote the
allegorical reality hoax
History Lesson Part II, the Minutemen, recorded at Radio Tokyo Studios, Venice, California
released July 1984,
Operating manual for self-driving car Earth
History except every time someone says 'history' it gets faster
spinning in fractals away from the anti-anti-antiauthoritarian left
'if your name is Heinemann then why can't you speak German?'
too close for comfort kerosene soaked bamboo socks igniting
a barricade of burning habitat pillows
and specaloos spice -
did you know it's actually not vegan? just a time warp
glitch in the hippie/punk 11 year subculture solar cycle - *Mr Narrator, this is Bob Dylan to me*
Anthroposophy's Decade in Russia, communise hygge
solving the solving,

prefigurative despair funeral for the next
spectacular foray
having to hope beyond hope that the methodology is
the only fault line no end to fetishising
the ways we furiously type against reality and furiously
somehow continue to get out of bed
purely to spite everything
despite everything

THEY NO VISION SAW
(For Phil Ochs and Paul Bennewitz)

still alive policing man i am thinking about your pink
shins a lot, your shins, my feet, our collision, more feet
so satisfying to kick something which is
an idea, but still you are cheap stationary in this.
because what do YOU know about what
will return me to the hospital?
the hospital i was born in no longer
exists due to funding cuts
but there's still the big austerity-proof
hospital in the sky, the hospital
between this world as we know it
and most of this world as it is.

see the thing is
i can't respect anyone who can't provide
a tender council of rabid wolves and a violent
evergreen for my tangled bedsores
so fate irreversibly dictates that for you
you will have to be destroyed
as will i but hopefully
less totally,
the edges of my worms being more porous
than the edges of the worms of law enforcement.

the spiritual path is a burning blockade,
fighting progress not change
on the spiritual plane i will lose my glasses
and have to ask my co-passengers to stand
to help me find them
under the pleather seats or another
tongue
but i will do it with no shame and i will
learn a new way of seeking around myself and others.
i cultivate infinite love and hate to balance

you, cop, cannot talk to me about this
even handed at the moment of impact
because i seem to offer it clearly but i just love to lie
when it's all really true and i can tell you everything
because you don't know shit, you don't know my shit,

you probably don't even know your shit,
your small intestine your gut flora? imagine - are
you there yet? picture your income after tax
divided by the lost dreams of your mother's maiden name -
got it? okay so it's like that but you even more
need it to live and valorise

did you become a cop to investigate UFOs?
i am trying to fertilise our common ground
but i am not sure who would die first or want
to, we know we know i understand i know all
about protection charms daintily tied to political positions
there's a violent cantankerous decorative approach
that seems necessary for my kind to survive yours

how did it feel when you killed phil ochs and did
you even know that summer existed? or paul bennewitz
unfortunately it makes no difference because as
much as you are stationary you are also no pilot
so you don't need to know about the existences of
blank spaces, after all, there's nothing there for a reason

they have no evidence that asylum Europeans or Eastern seekers are responsible for reported reductions in the swan population

Dank entrails folding into soft soups of hope where Dank entrails folding into soft soups of hope is a more nourishing than disturbing mental image to place deep inside someone   Where fences feeling nothing but playful obstacle courses linked or the deep blossom folds on the edge of skin elements of refusal beaten out but still   present in living horses, nobody wins the victory dance   Holding out for this   feeling hand shadow puppet of a hare twitching on the side of an empty bell tent   bright with candles waiting for its best life, best fire hazard beyond twee fascist incidentals   When is earth capitalised? Stare at the white interior all you want   if it's all you want but this failing drawing of a log cabin is   the hypothetical freedom of a place where there is no choice to be forced between anti-monarchism and swan adoration   Where all actions are tissue from a huge fucking desirable scar of intentionality away from the empty-full morning after drunk state of the honest answer to 'Where does your food come from?'   being 'Everywhere, so excuse my fragmented thought patterns, but I really write best when I am sad and fat with food from everywhere in the world   Cultured vulture for the last scraps of empire leaking sort of justified apocalypse anxiety manifest in a cupboard of thousands of lentils   the intrinsic conceptual excess of 'condiments' and the expectant capture of wild yeast   Do we need anything from the shop?' We might be out of milk forever Angry cages sucking each other dry yet social relations cemented with agave or high-fructose corn syrup, life or death   empty calories, social justice means civil war In a happier temporal zone the beehive mesh crawling with beetles fucking orchids - nothing abject about it - gesamtkunstwerk, darling   Medical/pastoral problems I am thinking about jerking off to after reading the NHS health page on paranoid thoughts, not because I'm into it but because I'm scared and thinking of attempting MEAT UNITED again   But I am a lazy coward so I write this instead, extra-nervous shaking and bleeding and my neck skin is kind of peeling off like I am a giant chubby pink snake with an anxiety disorder who can't even shed a fucking skin properly   It's all very boring like how I can never breath in the usual way you probably know all too well too and hopefully we'll do something about it one day because it's fucked up when thought about, feeling this close to alarm clock 24/7 when we could be chasing semi-domesticated pigeons around the nature reserved by the M25 ring road until I wheeze up something better than black phlegmy stale air Caught tight against the feeling that maybe I will be reincarnated as a lobster after London has flooded, that maybe I will find a nice rock formation to squat near Victoria Park roam a marginally less contested expanse of margin scribbling space in Hackney again angry androgynous teenage lobster with a bottle of Buckfast and a Conflict logo stencilled on their shell See the absurd temporalities I have to imagine and species boundaries I have to cross to roll out of bed and put one claw in front of the other? My politics are i hate the sky and send my love to the worms in the throne room, oh god fearing termites against the institution and the thin line between words and despair and teeth ground down to mustard yellow road markings Intersecting tubes masquerading as function destroyed by five thousand dandelions Endearing chronic faith condition shrink-wrapped vegetable soup, what is not infrastructure? If you're the company you keep I'm my ectoparasites - undoubtedly the first invertebrate metazoan to visit the underwater ley lines Know Your Mind Assess your paranoia You Can Be Happy The old utopian enemy There are people right now experiencing the movement of other people as a flux of targeted spiritual catastrophes, in some valid and some terrible ways No meat contained The sterile disgust of a scare story mercilessly eating souls churning out aspecific middle England's hellscapes so unbearably unbearably sad and desperate Honda Civic.

BATHS SUCK BUT THE STATE DOESN'T

Baths suck clearly in the sense of washing sucks in the sense of speculative nostalgia for my crusty new age traveller lifestyle BUT also in the sense of the clear necessity of reframing sucking   as a positive - the earth sucks but the state doesn't   Roots suck but the state doesn't   You suck but the state doesn't   I suck but the state doesn't   Sucking off the state sucks BUT the state sucking you off sucks more   In November 1982 Françoise d'Eaubonne wrote "It's not a question of integrating homosexuals into society, but of disintegrating society through homosexuality"   In September 1987 Thatcher declared 'There is no such thing as society' (it's not a misquote, it's much worse) and attacking her four years before this the punk band CRASS had said 'There is no authority but yourself' and somewhere in this constellation everything was disintegrating stagnant and upwards into shinier unfreedom some We (white homoetc.uals) integrated into that disintegration grabbed rainbows   and put them on flags and concentrated those flags in a small geographical area of an urban metropolis and called for more cops on the streets and called it a culture   <   Someone get me a fucking umbrella to protect against the UV of umbrella identity formations BUT maybe the condition of rainbow flags is paradoxically appropriate inasmuch as it is flat congelation of what is actually a trick of the light kinda deception by nature vibes like us babe-mate spectrum person Sexuality as subculture as religion as   All subcultures are religious in nature I'm having a 2008 crash I mean I'm into you I mean I like like you   inasmuch as you or I is a stable category beyond   an accumulation of coping mechanisms and sirens   came repeatedly all night long pre-empting the condition of man in the state of future   bungalows curled around the air the nation state is a tacky aesthetic unable to manufacture enough bunting to cover its own guts and always others blood   What happens when the god is undeniably objectively omnipotent and omnipresent but you don't believe in it? Finance capital fucks the skyline with blessings from its own skygods that only escape from becoming   not   everyone's with adequate alternatives   'adequate' alternatives being the kind that cannot peacefully co-exist   I mean when it is adequate it won't be the alternative and   What The Alternative Is An Alternative To will be a smouldering mountain of dead infrastructure good for nothing but decomposting   There it is, right, yeah, there that inherent contradiction leading to final battle that is the source of so much story I've yet to purge my sorry throat   Yet again me and some banker called Jeffrey reduce the inherent contradictions of capital to a fantasy roleplaying game - this is a bad affinity affinity   anyway enough about masculinity, but wait actually - Who or what is invited to the chemsex party? Who or what is invited to the moral panic? Who or what is always already chemsex party moral panic?   No interruptions for 1 hour / Indefinitely not so much a country as a storage facility On Canvey Island there is a high butcher's apron to local butcher ratio   a sign saying HOLE HAVEN   a sign saying LIQUID STORAGE FACILITY a metal watersnake swims out into the estuary presumably once for bringing gas to   ships to bring   power to a thing called 'culture'   or some shit like that but more easily assimilated into the body which ambivalently somewhat encompasses Canvey Island but also ships to London where one day chemsex parties will use electricity but also literally everything where does one draw the line at different scales of power? Is this history or narrative structure or just   The potential in everyone who is more scared of the world not ending (in a kinetic potential energy way not a coalition way)   All my embarrassing desperate appeals to a natural collective body   Aren't we all a little bit the Unabomber? The soul is complicit   ideal landscape is pure surplus an infinitely expanding carpark expansion expansion governmentality fetish party   The hexes inherent to your birth-assigned socio-economic grouping vs The hexes picked up along the way Assigned 'continuation of the species' at birth Boring terror I refuse to buy low-fat anything   You call me a fucking pagan for faith in holistic yogurt culture and so this is as far as we get   Chaos magic is neoliberal in its emphasis on individuality and its avoidance of the importance of collectively generated meaning   and community but how to spiritually nourish oneself from the collective knowledge of a community that does not and cannot exist yet? Or ever?   A bloody tooth stuck in organic sourdough bread at least feels honest   Last summer I got in an argument in a sauna with someone who said she would hate to edit my work because I use or maybe *am*   too many forward slashes and apparently the new narratives of the coming collapse or white flight or whatever must be formally grammatically correct   Make sure your curse items are easily biodegradable Anyway Each bus number assigned a card from the major or minor arcana CAUTION: HOT LIQUID CAUTION: HOT LIQUID CAPITAL sheer sudden drop / keep away from small children / You are my favourite choking hazard / Food as theological structuring principal // ASHES TO ASHES AND DUST TO DUST / / DEAD'S NOT DEAD AND PUNK'S NOT PUNK/ stuck at the tyranny of structures / the body's authority issues ultimately dwarfing all attempts at mediation by liquid safety packages 'i don't want to feel full of life, i want life to feel full of me' Disgusted we died loudly sometimes to drown out the sound of the neighbours fucking foxes the identity politics of an immaculate mason jar / green juice balanced on immigration enforcement What comes after the false hope of patchouli?

The Head is a Headless Hunter

the pole star is not a star
but in fact a role to be played
so i send in a cv to orion
(the best boss is a headless boss)
with a photo

of the inside of my eyelid
and an address: i live below
where the insides of the marshmallows
are now vacuums
'they' want

to build a road under stonehenge
i am praying for an ancient alien
cargo cult curse to bring the whole
fucking thing fucking crashing
down to earth

praise the sun
burn the sun
bumblebees appear
bumblebees appear on the endangered species list
good news becomes sterilised on contact with air, no risk

CAREER
substitutes COMMUNISM
substitutes CONTENTMENT
substitutes NOURISHMENT
substitutes NOTHING

drinking ice cream hot chocolate despite
the advice of my horoscope sorry my
nutritionist sorry my brain chemistry
because my guts can digest dairy better than despair or
they can't but there's only one way to find out

'what if it turns out my only real contribution
to the discourse is purely social lubricant?' i ask
my imaginary friend's dog, whilst offering
a shredded copy of the revolution
of everyday life as bedding

everything and everyone good* including
and especially the imaginary gets crushed
a red flavour slushy of hopelessness
articulation can't avoid
the asterisk after good

nothing is good i became so zen last year
it doesn't matter what i feel when i say
everyone good i am saying everyone
terrified of the sorting of people into
good and not good

Full Catastrophe Living at the end
of my fingertips, mushrooms
the cosmos, post-snow sludge
rotting roots, a future filled
to spilling with quietly religious engineers

there is no happiness
but just about this handful
of schoko-müsli washed down
with golden milk to keep
the fear moist and heavy empty crumble

the edible biopolitical sphere
the palm oil milk chocolate world egg
ate the toy inside to learn to be a
social digestion capable entity
of course i can read helvetica

exposure and response
prevention therapy
i spill my guts
it's all gravy
soaking into your absorbent bureaucracy

it is impossible to know how much of my creative process is
aerosol fumes or throwing stones
at the sans serif of the collective unconscious
alien abduction fantasy roleplay
stop using gendered pronouns for extra
terrestrial life

never trust a person without disgusting bodily habits
a shrine to their belly-button fluff house full
of menstrual blood filled pot plants
zombie fag end cigarettes
have you no joy left to eat
out of your nose?

another empty threat to disappear

The snapped-up wing   bone of a
rotting rat becomes divine inspiration
for the forward thinking branding of the new coffee shop
'it was just so   real'
Unambiguously pleasant
things are always well-presented violence's latte

Pro-people who wear black and thought or think
        they are going to end the world as it is
anti-people who wear black and   never or don't want to
hang the last graphic designer with the guts
                        of the last fitness blogger
nothing personal, we've abolished the personal, just a foray
against featureless despair bullet-pointed
against your filtered collarbone's vanilla
crawling with imagination's fun
bruises you won't acquire
There's no way to bruise capital despite
all the episodic nerve endings and
                              blue zinc blood private pools
and lack of filtration and drainage
surplus and
and

Dogs could do so much better
than us

I made a hole in my earlobe and it became
                rapidly expanding scab GOD
what do i have to do to escape metaphor
                  around here?   say a prayer
who cares. some words slip into the
                                        fungi's peripheral vision
ugh the worst spores
rose lemonade sidles up into the gap
in the arms of acceptance of the current one
    more cup of tea - refracted myopia door
bell chimes arrhythmic pulse deadening pastel uncoloured
                some more words go here, covered in Cath Kidston

lead weights underlying terror for the banal
constantly flowing cappuccino of existence and sub-
bourgeois malaise enacting
one hundred cute craft projects to try this
autumn, one hundred cute
lambs to sacrifice every autumn
before you die or
the void gets carpal tunnel syndrome
one year spent carving a mobile marble
stone monument to my unpaid invoices
and ryanair receipts
yeah, it's called an object based practice
and we all have one
yeah, it's called eating and shitting and talking around
those things and how you sustain them
like they're not the main event
and it's not relevant how

the poem makes sense because it is
too ugly for other career paths
the poem makes sense all day long
then goes home and scours craigslist for alternative employment
the poem probably doesn't want to get paid
to watch you clean naked
or make you a costume for burning man
but maybe it wouldn't be so bad

all i ever wanted was a pink heirloom potato and late capitalism
wouldn't give it to me
(or at least, the means, i mean)
weightless metal sculpture
sorry
subculture
i love the decorative and i hope he's doing okay, it's tough out there

the revolution is my boyfriend
my boyfriend is an airport departure lounge
the airport departure lounge is my subculture
i am cooking a badger over an open fire in the perfume department
on the verge

of closeness of constantly on the tender verge
of a tax return deadline on the sun-bathed verge

of a suburban arms factory on the embittered verge
of the simmered down lack of freshly ground spring
bluebell fields leaking into the jasmine horizon uncontainable
but no
no base catharsis
just a policeman and
a line of text
&
another policeman and
another line of text

but wait before you leave! -

the word of the day is

generosity

same as yesterday

i love a cyclical
redemption
narrative

Defiance County, Ohio

a torture fantasy of useful suffering a friend tells me
they have noticed me going through a church phase
if you have to try it's not real love i mean repentance
no Protestant work ethic to speak of or answer to

i don't believe in regional personality trait essentialism
but i will also never be
a cool New York poet who
reads
slowly
for a reason -
there are too many brisk terrors to give false names to

i gave the list of names to the police force the
force that we abolished, remember when?
we took on globalisation and won
free meat and drink and cloth

letters biting statistics cavernous fertilised torrents
there's no page to turn, history forgot to
compartmentalise. how is history gendered if
it can't multitask? all we know is the answer,
another insipid misogyny against leviathan

the absolute world spinning on its absolute
self and me bc what axis and stupid
punks laughing on the night bus I want
to believe and the pain of their laughing
and grunts when I thought better could
happen and deep depressions on the earth's
crust and fight war not wars

constantly dragged away from the cliff
drop into warm squishy sleep lavender
and bath salts and always the lunatic fringe
my methodology doesn't exist yet, i was
handed a Proper Noun and quest at birth
All Motions Are Perpetual

living the dream living the folded
pinecone of my brain cells
neatly stacked fractal of the wider
discursive despair blackening church

happy slippage into the anti temporal
numb age i don’t want to know how
we got here how we stencilled something
actual on the sky a circled A chemtrail
freudianship plain stained orange magenta
writing thru the terror and relentlessly
unconsistant avocado production
instead of weirder homes and gardens
we’re all gonna die for golf courses

visualisation: you are a small shark in the aquarium in the office of the CEO of a nondescript corporate body in a mid-80s postmodern swirl carpeted disaster zone where all the glass is cleaned except yours, the day is broken with elevator music but you don't know this is what this is. You are nibbling on some plankton and waiting for communism and you write a poem on the discretely moulding moulded glass of your aquarium. the poem reads:

the perfect sphere of commonality made up of direct lines in direct
contradiction to the present circum-
stantial scratching the hollow surface of liquid soluble anxiety
a great swarm of bees pollinate the edges of the
deserted sub-genre is anything ugly
or beautiful enough to be the
rupture of the skin on the
milk of global geopolitical
catastrophied muscle?

like most people, the earth just gets hotter with age

can i pay my rent in social niceties? is there an open bar or
promise of a consensual collective solution for the spiritual
crisis of western modernity - cheap white wine is a safer
bet but just get me whatever can still be salvaged
where is ecstasy on the food chain in relation
                                        to obligation? we are
getting cooler and cooler, despite this you cave in and look
                                        at a recent picture of the world
wow they really did get really hot.

a gay hare is walking through a forest - in case you don't
                    know, a hare is a butch rabbit
i don't want to be defined by my sexuality i'm just a human
says the hare

the forest's infrastructure is devastated by Dutch elm disease,
which is not the point it's just also happening in the world
          near the point
outside the harsh city limits of
                    the point is everything that constitutes
the periphery
leaks into the centre, the centre is undeserving of the
bioluminescence

at the centre of the octopus

sneak in an oblique reference to roaming swarms of trauma
in the form of fluorescent yellow and black and white checked
lines separating you from you from not-you, the potential
at any moment to be reminded that there is no sovereignty
and sovereignty is a value that lubricates the social and
membership is declined all the time when the noise and the love-

you shouldn't anticipate anticipation's anticipation
no dessert until you finish your labour
you're not an octopus, you're a shark
you have better things to do than draw yourself new clocks
the calendar just works, get over it

make narrative fate again

stop trying to wrap your slimy tentacles around the world
and reinvent sliced bread and get back
to being a shark

i learnt everything i know about politics
and economics sitting in a tank of finite water
and never sleeping without also moving
and watching the world from the outside
and our time will get even even
if nobody ever cleans this glass
get even even if

Situationist International Airport

a glittering situationist internale blackpool
or truthfully closer to pre-gentrified margate finally
relief from the beige moralistic combine harvester
matching androgynous smock connotations of
our politic in the popular imagination finally
meta-maoist disco at the crumbling roller rink red linoleum
the modernist victorian holiday resort glamour we were
promised by our avant guarded bearded bespectacled
ancestors of the concrete poetry may 68 glitz
neon signage above the chip shop the promiscuity we were
prophesied not free love actual sex the whole real sometimes
not great great thing greasy frying smell of killing
alienation and burnt sugar popcorn the epicentre
of our culture as explained by the older boys who knew
about debord so debonair and anti-bourgeois
bourgeois sophisticated and now we are
through this bleak crystal sea side town that is ours
through a portal it has always been ours even
before history before we knew we needed it
a pier full of benjamin's arcades, but not like that
like if benjamin had designed arcade games
on hashish and the whole town is stalked by a big
cat which is to say a big cat sized cat that is
just a cat but wild and haggard and hungry
for the taste of capitalist blood and i am a young man
cruising the charity shops full of comme des garçon
and spring/summer 1916 hugo ball cardboard and
floral abbie hoffman drapery i make meaningful
eye contact and before i know it i am
being told to sleep outside the family
home next to the patio heater for being queer
and i think about shouting back to my
idiosyncratically reactionary family
'do you know where we live??'
but instead shout back
'i don't even need to live here!
i earn a million pounds a year!'
so business must be good
in situationist international blackpool

according to wikipedia i am in the 'initial struggle for success' phase of my life as bruce springsteen's life

oi i only listen to experimental noise music
made by people who have
what i deem interesting
enough subject positions
because i'm a leo moon dickhead w a gay agenda
but i'm not all that
bad because other people
wash vegetables with soap; besides
i always can walk around the supermarket if ever i want to
listen to the experimental noise
music of the straight
white world at checkout number 4 please
no clues towards any higher resolution
of this
'after the revolution'
all hail the new water purifier!
we meet the mind-body
halfway down the water slide
the soul screams elsewhere in the plastic tubing
george michael on hampstead heath
predictable turbulence above the bay of biscay
i clutch my pearl necklace of steroid cream
wince at accidentally thanking another border cop
but i'm willing to think of anything as psychosomatic
stars were exploding abscess
chant in my head and pray
a-anti-anti-histamina! a-anti-anti-histamina!
causative or curative; regardless i stick
a fluorescent cocktail
umbrella in my brain
the only promised land i believe in
is springsteen's
socialist homoerotic butch americana
i organise a cocktail soiree
for all the world's great living poets
and all the footballers and criminals and crime victims
who share their names
and beat their search engine rankings
get on the floor

nobody move
or respond to any work-related emails
        no value
just pina coladas

Depression Calculator

i can't be ideological about my happiness even though happiness
is entirely ideological it is one of those things like buying popcorn
at the cinema i hate to be the bearer of bad happiness news i
wanted the 20th century to sort it out too but sadly that is not
in stock right now this unabridged cynicism is not very me but
unfortunately that's me i recently discovered this while getting
drunk on frozen margaritas with my high horse that everyone i
never listened to knew how to live better all along but that was
two long months ago so now i am ready to get a homophobic
straight edge hardcore band tattoo on my forehead like i really just
want to get radicalised and commit stop pickpocketing the culture
for the subculture and see the forest for the bulldozers the problem
with the drives to inclusion or exclusion is we're all already the
same thing we're just bad at being it

TRAVEL DIARY SUMMER 2016

Let's work for wild life. It would be good for me, you know. It would. Getting up early I mean rising with the sun I mean rising with the cockerel I mean writing with the ticking thermostat and working with the mind in the ocean stage. The stage before the rivers and streams of consciousness run up their respective mountains and valleys, you know it's one of the first traumatic separations of the day, that sort of spike when you are really no longer dreaming and you check your clock because there is again a time that it really can just be, and some shape of carbohydrates to eat to maintain something like a cohesive form. It's the future it's the past it's geographical specificity it's the circle of life and stolen bikes it's trying to get my tongue so deep into my cheek that it reaches my heart. Past the burning barricade behind my skull, inbetween my eyes, the third eye stress headache that occurs when reincarnated summit-hopping black bloc congregate in my forehead to make me sweat anxiety and shame as I walk around the supermarket. It's good, knowing there's some small rodent still left breathing steadily, keeping warm amongst the glowing coals. Dreamt I got a tattoo reading 'fuck novelty' that I only show on special occasions. Not really. But really, keep beauty intact and fragmented. The thought that counts is terrifying. You should always eat raw garlic for a sore throat, I don't know if it works but you'll feel better.

Broken safety curtain reading: British public wrong about nearly everything. Smouldering pit of red, white and blue snakes eating each other into circles in the fiery depths of Hull. Airborne disease manifests dissatisfaction at the state of all that is yet to come, fallow and pristine faux-marble, they won and we didn't smash enough. Never enough. Just left a compacted lump of all the worst of the world. What can feral disgust eat in the face of sterile misery? Enacting an empty-handed shrug of an apology for constant undulating preemption of more of the same. Health and safety gone mad, health and safety goes mad and is referred for a course of CBT and gets back to work. How many silver-winged falcons would it take to lift the room out of its current context? Once you get onto an MOD site, could take you anywhere.

The places it is hard to feel like anything is wrong cooked close with the places it is hard to feel like anything is not. Weather forecasting is a boom industry. Sometimes the world gets too much and too full and sometimes I fall out of it, or leave to a quieter place and forget my keys and get stuck sitting on the doorstep outside the world waiting for someone, or something, to let me in. Then I wrote down my future (now current) address.

Terrified of everything that scientists 'have no idea what causes,' hoping for comfort in the spectre of causality, causality as bare minimum of bodily autonomy. My anxiety levels get up and stay hard for hours with this one weird tip. Community gardens are my happy place within all this. Fantasising about crawling around on all fours in Görlitzer Park and barking at the other dogs, but unlike most of the other dogs I have a relatively hairless human form that is externally indistinguishable from me, and must carry my paternalistic hierarchical self-designated best friend around in my head, and present to the world as such. Someone tells me Hegel's only poem was about being a dog, but this means very little to me, because I am a dog. Also, I am meeting a woman I don't know for for ice cream. Retrospectively, it rains and there is no ice cream. Unfortunately, scientists really have no idea what causes lycanthropy.

I want to be a werewolf and all gardens to be community gardens and community to be a dead word and for the clouds to blow over before ice cream I want to stop fighting weather and I want an unmarked landscape punctuated by small settlements characterised by continual unconditional care beyond biological familial ties I want to be a big fluffy puppy that looks like me as a big fluffy puppy and retains my earnest enthusiasm for food and play but loses the neurosis that I (like all animals) have developed as a result of co-habitation with humans. Sometimes I am that puppy but it is getting harder and harder. Unsure if stubborn northern European commitment to sitting in barely summer parks is an encouraging desire to connect with the earth come whatever may, or bourgeois excess. Probably both. The English radical tradition rolls off my tongue with warm moist familiarity because the English radical tradition is inherently reactionary. I google 'folk session berlin'. The differences between being a reactionary and having a critique of progress are the subjectivities and aesthetics of the people who like you and the people who hate you. I could make a strong case for why techno is folk but it's not going to make me feel better today.

I want to savour the taste of bone in my mouth with no concept of species or anatomy, oh to be fucking respectability against a wall and lost bounty and a thousand empty grapes, just to unsatisfy them when they pay someone to peel you empty. Nothing is not a metaphor. Any similarities to real infrastructure, living or dead, are purely coincidental. If I could as a demonstration of the gravitational pull of places that feel like home, I would insert [picture of the sun-drenched bank of this river that is really a canal I don't yet have a name for and the crickets and birch trees and knotweed thriving under this motorway flyover, connected by the semi-irregular landscaping rocks that attempt to make landscapes of the lands in between that are specifically and intrinsically not landscapes]. Imagining my dick to be these two landscaping rocks and a piece of chipped plywood sitting a few feet away from me, more landscaping rocks and dehydrated grass scrub sustaining the somatic connection. Last month I lost my glasses because I was so excited to swim in the sea I forgot that part of why it looked so sharp and sparkly and perfect was that I was wearing my glasses. The plywood dick is about six inches long, I signed up for Grindr yesterday, I lied and said I was pre-hormones as if such a linear trajectory is in motion, as if anyone is pre-hormones. I want gender reassignment surgery to be a shitty stick-and-poke ACAB tattoo.

Feels necessary to say how disgusted I am by the very literal and unambiguous I situation in this work, maybe inherent to the 'travel diary' form. Recommended that a guy I might have been on a date with (nobody knows) that he should buy Close to the Knives by David Wojnarowicz, instead of I Love Dick by Chris Kraus. He did, and the shopkeeper complimented him on his choice, and I wanted to be like 'I told him to get it!' The I really is really terrible a lot of the time.

I actually think capitalism is quite a beautiful word and look forward to appropriating it to mean something like spring dawn sunshine ladybird sex. While trying to meditate out of severe dissociative symptoms, I keep coming back to the possibility of undiagnosed Lyme disease, but also the fact that the only conversations I am really invested in are food, weather, and dreams, and how they are commonly cited as the most boring conversations, and this feels like a question of what is too bodily to be worthy of intellectual consideration and what is pristinely abstract enough to not get dragged down into the bowels and skin of the conversation? Maybe the reason people feel there is nothing exciting to say about food and weather and dreams is that they can feel that everything to be said about them already exists pulsing through all matter, in every body, every cell, every star, so words are sunken fossils in the face of the wonder of it all. I never feel like this, and I am constantly desecrating with my attachment to description, always getting distracted by the oil slick on the surface of the conversation. This is what I meant about it being hard to be a big fluffy puppy that looks like me. The fundamental pathos is that I am an earth sign in high-performative drag as an air sign. That's why the CO2 infused nettles and rosehips of places like this work. There is right here the whole progression of infrastructure, the canal forced into redundancy by the motorway and the planes overhead, and I can be in all that comforting abstraction, stick fluorescent post-its on the cracked concrete for citation purposes, and come home with dirt on my thighs.

Desire doesn't feel like a significant mental paradigm for me, being mostly driven by anxiety, and I saw this as a sad but potentially lucky escape before realising that anxiety might just be the negative imprint of desire and as usual, there is no escape. Read an article about how people were overcoming their anxiety by telling themselves 'I'm excited.' Months before I read this, I had come to my own epiphany and been enthusiastically telling people 'I hate excitement! It's the same as anxiety.' Two types of people, I guess, reactionaries and those with a critique of progress.

There are people fishing further along, which is probably a bad idea, I mean they probably shouldn't eat the fish, but at this point I think that everything is so bad that it is essentially fine. Been feeling a kind of nihilistic surrender to the ubiquitously carcinogenic nature of the modern world, we all die of existing in the world, same as we always have. A woolly mammoth or castle siege or aspartame.

Must be frustrating for philosophers that the dumb world, I actually wrote word but I meant world, the dumb world spinning on its dumb axis is this much and this little fabric to make a winter jacket from. Just wrote REJOICE (all caps for the live audience) on my left (your right for the live audience) thigh, best time yet, maybe the permanent time (retrospectively not the permanent time, for the non-live audience).

People always ask me about the relationship between writing and art-making as if I ought to experience it as fraught. Nobody ever asks me about the relationship between art-making and gardening, which feels much more cognitively dissonant. Increasingly when I am very low and very nowhere I think in preparation for my future think piece about how I gave up a promising art career and found peace and spiritual fulfilment running an isolated rural goat farm in the Pyrenees, or wherever. It's not inevitable until you can't delay it anymore. I am going to get sunburn and worry about skin cancer out of habit, despite bravado and bold claims to the contrary, and eat comfort bread and get angry and pray for helpful dreams so I should probably go now

Bye

p.s. imagine a world without wild life

Better than Sex (For Simon Chapman)

Years later vague new friends lived on the same street in £550/month shared housing which was one of those things there was no way to legitimately be angry about, they were not really the ultimately global financial interests that removed the space from itself, they just lived there after, as I did also, in different places that by the time I got there might as well have been the same spaces. I went to a party at their house on NYE 2013/4 and thought *you don't even know about my birthday when Simon bit through his tongue on ketamine or you don't even know about me when i thought making soup with potatoes from a bin would change the world.* These events collapse into each other in their total removal from the disinfected space of the present time which scraped the mould off the walls and took down the sign warning about rats, painted over all the walls the colour people paint things when their goal is to paint something anything, rather than make it any particular colour. To my frontal cortex everything is pale green sludge cut with dusty sunlight on a Saturday morning, cycling through the last years of Hackney as it corresponds to my felt sense of that landmass as a maternal figure. The crusty semiotics of the kitchen, the way all squatter punk house kitchens smell the same everywhere in Europe, Liz Cook charts with herbal remedies and seasonal vegetables as a laminated wallpaper backdrop for subsisting on skipped Pret- A-Manger sandwiches and Polish lager (because it's vegan - this was the era of being told 'Did you know most beer isn't vegan?' at least 10 times at every party, an era I assume to be ongoing somewhere), my best guess at the smell is generic curry power plus patchouli plus eco washing up liquid plus never quite scrubbing the spilt Tyskie thoroughly enough. It's kind of the best smell in the way that whoever you're fucking is kind of the best smell even when the part of your brain that doesn't matter (which is mostly other people) says it's objectively not. Get a shower! Get a job! Someone shouts at me to get a job and I shout back that I am *literally* still at school, which I usually hate to say but love to say in that moment. Some bands are gonna play later and someone says enthusiastically 'One of them is actually pretty good!' My aesthetic is haute couture temporal drag, floral Doc Martens with red and black laces, black military surplus with a CRASS logo stencilled on the back and FIGHT WAR NOT WARS and I am a time traveller true believer to be petted on the head and fussed over by the ones who did not time travel but had remained continuously from the source culture I imagined to be somehow intrinsic, something in the water, until the water became coconut water and I found out how expensive generic vegan slop could become, and then all that is left is to fight the notion of this as inevitable or progress or inevitable progress.

Occasionally I still haunt my old haunts, burn my mouth on a pre-party vegetable samosa, which is no longer stomach lining but a metaphysical comfort ritual of the continuity of something amidst constantly encroaching plate glass windows. The man behind the counter whose name I have never known and who has never known either of mine, although he has known me for ten years and at least three genders, asks where I've been, why it's been so long, the answers get further and further apart - 'I'm not around here so much anymore' - 'I moved to South London' - 'I live in Berlin now' - whenever I make the pilgrimage back, there's the fear of not being the one who has moved. Walking through Mariannenplatz with the only friend here old enough in relation to me to have also known Simon, we reminisce about how he was one of the good ones, how welcoming he was to us both, the implicit understanding of that as something of an exception. We talk about fascism and the black bloc and the G20 *again* and the German left and what is to be done while we look for the right tree to piss behind. I remember Simon telling me about the Poll Tax Riots, or maybe J18, and saying 'That moment, when the crowd turns and it kicks off, it's better than sex!' and my 15 year old self nodding sagely like I understood what it all meant.

the reverse of a ramification is buttered toast

i have to believe if i drink enough chamomile tea, maybe five litres, then nothing can touch me, my tendons, not a glance not a history not a gender nothing just the nest i call a bed i have been reading r.d. laing and i think predictably it was a bad idea i tell my therapist i don't want to have to be anything and i am scared to lose the magical worldview that destroys and sustains me and i am scared that that is what 'better' looks like but i am also scared of going insane i have to remain on the right side of *choosing* to ignore the consensus whilst still hyperaware of its tepid little mechanisms acting upon me he says we are getting into abstract territory i say this *actually* is my kitchen then i go to a lover's house and they say they want to see my sculpture and i say i am self-conscious about my making practice at the moment because it doesn't exist and we listen to post-punk and hit each other round each other's faces and it is all exactly what i want for this present condition's staccato of an apocalypse until the bathos of the spotify advert corrupts our bowels with laughter and they say 'don't stop, that's what *they* want' and i agree somewhat except i don't know if *they* ever want us to laugh or if laughter is inherently more or less marketable than an affectionate right fist to the left shoulder or if by the point of awareness of the problem it is already too late then it is always already too late which is why i have given up trying to get up before 10am, i love talking about sex to straight audiences so everyone gets interpolated into my fantasy like they try to do to me every day i want to stress the inherent contradictions and incompatibilities of our desiring worlds, it's a wet war but a war none the less, if you are wondering what the sides are, one of them is when my friend fanny said 'i am not at all ambitious, if it was up to me all i would do is read novels and fuck' and i thought that is the greatest ambition of all, that is the side i will place all my most valuable possessions on, then there is the other side which is simply the enemy who gets enough bandwidth already so i will not elaborate, as much as it is in my nature to do so ever since i realised the amount of ornamentation i wanted to inflict on the world ever since i realised i was a delicately carved negative relief of everything i hated in the world it was a fantastic moment i get an email from a stranger asking if i would like to submit to a conference about artistic working practices and the money is good so i think of all the things i could say about non-work work for some of that money and then i think about how the only reason i showered today was so i could stop thinking about our hands in each others mouths long enough to work and also because i didn't really feel like my fellow customers in netto necessarily deserved the smell of us and i needed chocolate also to compensate for work never less than 70% cocoa because answering emails when you could be reading novels and fucking is terrible

where am i supposed to access the commons to grow the language
or soft wheat to fill the gendered gaping hole in the middle of
the dinner table fresh pansies, rosemary and thyme from our
non-garden a seeping sage bush actor theory jewish diasporas
heritage: massive lack of language for joy as equal to complaint
the negative is an infinite rose garden for the positive we eat
the roses and say 'this is great, thanks for cooking!' or 'nothing
beats fresh asparagus!' or 'what are you doing later? i realised i
left my bike and john wieners book at yr house - we could make
food or something?' in a shoe shop in england everyone was
saying goodbye constantly, trying to imagine a revolutionary
imaginary when all clouds essentially look like mashed potato - i
wish i was as happy rn as this naked-apart-from water-wings
toddler having a screaming tantrum but i have been ghosting my
therapist and when i reply and finally break the radio silence, he
replies 'Whoop! Whoop!' so i guess he's happy i'm not a ghost
is there such a thing as a revolutionary dinner table? last supper
at the end of history there is, like, no sun there is like no sun
there is like no son no, archetypal sun, you can't go there take
your lips off his the proverbial contemporary anxiety waxing
poetic attempts all i mean really is fuck the world for making me
asthmatic reflective non-production reflective non-production
reflective non-production reflective non-production reflective
non-production reflective non-production honestly i'm not copy
and pasting, i love labour, reflective non-production reflective
non-production the first line of my cv is i am really fucking scared
of the dark so that everyone knows i have a good imagination and
am therefore a great artist, i am scared of the dark please buy my
work i am scared of the dark i feel the archaic dark forces rising
from the corners of my bedroom the carpet curls up a thousand
owls a thousand ghouls a thousand unknowns my houseplants
turn to triffids and tear at the foundations of the structure the
triffid of asbestos i left facebook again that great eater of souls
i'm not melodramatic it's just thursday afternoon i'm anxious
about my anxiety the world is a click the world is a simulation
according to people playing it on easy mode, nobody makes it out
alive but let's make out alive i love to write poems i love to eat
carbohydrates i love my tomato plants the allotment on the front
lines burning our ikea dinner table because fascism it's not violence
it's not against people it's against an ikea dinner table and it's
al consequences, my household's food crop this year so
toes approximately 2cm in diameter each

A pause to glare at the person next to me in the cafe who just laughed whilst saying 'failed utopia'

almost 1 decade before this 1 i poured triple distilled optimism
into unfilled water
bottles and tried to snuck them past security and successfully done
so throw it up metabolised into the cracks in the paving stones
i didn't want to live unless i changed the world
and then i did and didn't

we must devastate the avenues where the avenues live
blood moon & the beached city explodes on impact with it
selves under- definitions
nothing is two dimensional but nothing doesn't
help, only serves
to admonish the underbelly further for their failure to not be
at least on the side of sides

there is a jagged flock of songbirds procrastinating
in the boughs between what is
and what could unbitterly be
tearing holes in the fabric of nothing's life-force
skin breaks down skinny break down infinite causality scroll
i don't have eczema because i'm stressed i have eczema
because i hate everything projected
outwards but my forcefield is weak

might have burnt down a ski lodge to the ground but instead
got myself red raw seeping skin
after all these people
the body is one site of many
where the end of itself is the only possible source
of experiencing itself as possible

black military surplus with seven limbed sleeves
ready to attack the fragile centrepiece human mean
-ing there is no space left in on the table for dazzling
etiquette or meanness, a kind of hideous
taxonomy is emerging from the wreckage
of the organic apple orchard's geodesic dome

work is a palindrome and an occupational hazard i'm not
a futurist just hate the present neurology i get

as it exists as a result of the ideology of futurism
i'm not a futurist because of disdain for the present what
comes after the revolution we are before i hope neurology

not not didactic because things are fucked
up and need to end to experience themselves as limit—
-full potential and get their shit together
        together the collapsing horizontal
flattening of eating disordered taxonomy into generalised
contemporaneity the crusted brittle of anxiety's womb
chemistry shell physicality repulsing the physical

finding a place to be still in a world with free
market escalators is a piece of lego under a human foot forever
and paying for the privilege
the question mark expresses the limitation that allows
a sense of potential liberation?
the skin is an inverted question mark
what kind? lie back and think of the sunken isle

ignore latent exhaustion's knowledge
it might be the same smug trappings
no we don't throw parties, are you here for the afterparty
or the pre-afterparty? we won't know until after
the event is beginning

it was nobody's fault
nobody? AGAIN?
somebody should stop nobody. it's
okay there's no wi-fi beyond the fate, it's safer
than safe, sterilised stone zone type safe blanket

a prospective hits like a dull thud
a car hits a pheasant, not like a pheasant
coincidentally also involuntarily complicit victims
of the aristocracy
we are not really bourgeois enough (in the means sense) to shoot

pheasants, those emasculated dinosaurs
we just run them over
it's a position the earth picks me
out from between her teeth, spits me out, all is not
forgiven
and did or didn't

Theses on Land Masses (After Ian Hamilton Finlay)

How to think of anything like leaping revolution
in the monumentalised constant defying rupture
of the context of a garden, lose
some answers and compost them for next year

Everything is land somehow kept seaweed sculptures
apart, water is wet land, your bedroom is dry land, the
sound of crackling firewood on an illegal blue
bonfire is land, the gallery wall is worse
land, and sometimes least of all, at least in
terms of perceived value, the land is
land is land.

Tenants rights are land struggle, albeit Teflon
travelling is land struggle, existing
in public is land struggle, adblock
is land struggle, the micro-geographical
availability of flat whites and aperol
spritz is land struggle, who laughs
at that joke is land struggle, like
how finally and least importantly,
art is land struggle.

All the land is all the other land and a fence
between gates is really just another rusty
hinge in need of oil, but look where
that got us before? More war more gates! Oil
is fat and so who really needs oil except
those working on the land, oh but yeah,
I already said, it's all the land.

We all work the land but I am worried
of dying from all the time I spend sitting
writing poems on the land.

To invent life out of picaresque brevity
The revolution is digesting or,
it is bullshit.
There is no authority but your food source.
There is no authority but the ground -
utopian if true.

We have to believe one bad apple does not spoil the barrel,
and thousands of jailers do not spoil the shipping container.

It could be as simple as radically present bird
-watching without categorising, practising
breathing the world as a lazy tidal August
pistachio ice-cream. Relatedly, when something
is burnt to ash it creates the illusion of vanishing
spread too thinly across the earth's crust,
read Warhol as/via a property developer, 'land
really is the best art,' reconstitute a battle cry for the
destruction of both, interior brickwork and exterior colons
and their foundational wicker
structural principals, no direct implication
art must be the best land. Oh, for
garden shed socialism, why,
not?

The first day of May chews its fingernails, Post-capitalist
politics are inevitably out of date and fortunately
the politics of ecstatic grieving i.e.
composting, to stay grounded it is
important to measure the heat to avoid
E Coli.

My family of communists are mystics, that is my family
of mystics are gardeners, that is my family of gardeners
are communists, that is all my distant relative materialists
keep one foot in the cosmos, because where else
could the material come from? And of course, Marx
was a Taurus. To drag the heavy rocks of words like
REVOLUTION and HISTORY into the garden, and
leave them to grow lichen, and if left long enough
to crumble into the sands of time, work done. Work?

All land is fictional, this is both the problem
and a potential source of the solution. The ground is not
solid and never was and never will be, thankfully

Land has or is no essential morphology or
topography, but spectres often get stuck and energy
often circulates as an ouroboros, for better
and/or worse, there is hope in leakage and drainage

There is no pleasurable consumption under
capitalism, a more chestnut syrupy motivational than
'no ethical consumption under capitalism'
Destroy purity but leave a droplet behind to thrive
to make sure you've really destroyed purity.

Fuck ethics, that scratched non-stick pan we keep
using, fuck ethics in the way that 'destroy purity' i.e. leave
a little behind because otherwise how are you gonna
fuck ethics? A stone basilisk carved with the words
'FIRST SHARD OF GLASS FROM THE SMASHED
MCDONALDS WINDOW, W.T.O. PROTESTS,
DOWNTOWN SEATTLE,
NOVEMBER 30TH,
1999.'
Underneath, laid a wreath of amputated white dreadlocks,
softly simmering patchouli.

Under the paving stones, the soil. Gardening Situation
ism, the overgrown fringes of a viable sentence, the radical
fringe geraniums call upon the sky I call upon
the destruction of hetero-sexualised disdain for the past
conquered commonality and other nice sounding
in the mouth root formations

The satisfaction of the bitter fruits and relationships
and modes of being what we grow for ourselves, somber joy
and ecstasy's responsibility in our accountability in seeing

Shifting the emphasis from capital to
land is not inherently feudal
but there could be as many peasantries
as there are startups endlessly
proceeding to gate number 8 immediately.

Adorable pastoral avant garde inherited Capability,
or Lancelot the fatal flaw in the theses might be the
twee-eager bloomed pastel yellow chalk of poetry about gardens
stumbling over Futurisms fascist monopoly on writing architecture
and the metallic blood-in-the-mouth canon of food verbalising
thinking through origin, continuation and rupture of the
species.

There's no progress, progress will be total detachment
from the existing meaning of progress.
Revolution is crop rotation.

Food and death rule at both extremes
of happiness, food and death rule
everything around everyone.
'Cheer up, food isn't everything in life, you know.'
- The landlord's daughter, The Wicker Man, a
- slippage into the pre-Pagan post-Pagan
Christianity of Summer Isle before the crops
and one monolithic attempt at white culture
failed. Everything was woodland before
it was everything.

Food sovereignty is the finely chopped garlic
and onion of political struggle, especially indigestible
and lumpy when people forget and understand
it as eternally peripheral and sealed.
Everything is about food
Everything that is not land is food.
Food = energy = power - No shit.
Food = energy = ~~religion faith spirituality~~
~~ALL CROSSED OUT~~ the thing that sits
happy and lonely beyond all those things
Bit into the stones and they bit back alive
The mouth as portal to the spirit world
Spit as portal to the spirit world.
Spirit as portal to the spit world.
A world without shipping containers.
The world is a shipping container.
The world is a shipping container for unimaginable joy.
It's not pointless to decorate the interior.

The roomba bullies the cat and the cat
realises domestication was a faulty
bargain to start with even circulated redundancy.
Gardening the centre gradually erodes
the quality of the centre.

The ontology of the gate is eager to discover
it's dual purpose, alternative career
path as automatic pomegranate deseeder
or Christmas tree decorating ladder to be

removed from hibernation and loved
then discarded once per year.

Repetition is an island nation.

Force open a huge cavernous gap between
the senses 'of belonging' and 'of entitlement',
forget they ever shared a plot, ate in the same
restaurant, shared a bed and burgeoning family values.
Redistribute bodily good functioning to
account for accidents and blessings of birth
placard reading: APPLE CIDER VINEGAR.

Monsters grow thick and deeply slimy everywhere
and I want never to use them as an analogy for what
I might be against despite the unresolved hero complex
gifted to me by white hetero-judeo-christian theology.
I try to prove I is dislike them, the Eel
in the Sink.

Nature in the sickly pine air freshener fighting its discrete
privately commissioned battle against the zombie
economy of life, the shape of the pine tree as futility.
My newborn kombucha is in danger from the fruit
flies humming around my discarded coffee grounds, the rice
our estranged housemate left in the rice cooker
to go mouldy as protest, lest we forget all
mould is not equal.

After Gogol:
Colonisation of land always needs
dead souls, ownership of land always requires dead souls,
real or imaginary, ownership of
land is always ownership
of dead souls.

Remembrance Sunday and the month before
when any corpus not sporting a poppy corpus becomes
an affront to the national corpus, the preservation
of which led to the circumstances the poppy corpora
supposedly mourn.

How to force open the semiotic gap between a brilliant
spiteful red flower that thrives on disturbing soil and

insane fucking WI national heritage fascism decorative
soap suds? Tiny frosted glass shard stuck
in the foot of the wider population
own vast majority of the land

There is enough land
somewhere, which means everywhere
All religions are at least sometimes
earth-based religions, sage and parsley parted
religiosity, spared sterilised doctrine's fingers
ritualised heavier than ionised water dispersed air

I need to learn cooperation with the more sterilised airborne gods,
they need to get their sweatless paws away from
the hopes of the worlds and systems I love inside.
My angry herbal muscles revolt bringing the fertile
vapour fine, /example of privilege's muscle relaxation
the heartfelt battle for gut feelings.

The work of leaving and not
leaving and doing and not
doing enough and never even
left the front gate, somebody has
to bury the earth.

THERE IS NO USE, THE USE THERE IS
HAS CURLED ITSELF STEAMED AROUND
THE COMFORT FOODS OF THE WORLD
BLISTERED THE CLOVE AND GINGER
SCENTED HEARTH THAT AVOIDS SENTI
MENTALITY THROUGH BEING BATTLE
WON. A HOUSE BUILT OUT OF BOTTLED
WATER ANCESTRAL ORGAN MUSIC /
THE WAR FOR SOFT TISSUE ESCAPE
PLANS DRAWN ON THE BACK OF ESCAPE
PLANS. THE BEE HIVE OF MOTHER'S
TONGUE AND THE SOVEREIGN SOVERE
IGN MOP BUCKET THE OBTUSE FEAR OF
FINDING WRONG ADAPTATION ADAPTING
TO ACCEPTANCE ACCEPTING ADAPTABLE
OKAY-ING. SOUND SYSTEM. IT IS MUCH
LESS THAN THE SLIMEY ROCK THEORY
OF DNA THAT DOESN'T AVOID THE PIT
FALLS OF WHAT MIGHT BE DESCRIBED
AS UTILITY BUT WORKS BETTER WHEN
WORKING AS UNDESCRIBED AS

FRESH ROSES ON THE TABLE
SOMETHING LIKE SECURITY
FIRM REASSURANCE BAKED
CAKE WE WILL REPEATEDLY FUCK UP
NEL CASHMERE NEUTRALITY OF
BERATED ENFORCED CHEER TEAM
ANTIPATHY TO THE SUN
MEDITATE TOWARDS THE SKY
THE EARTH IS BETTER OFF WITHOUT
LABOUR OR VALUE OR RESPECT
MOUTH THE FUTURE
IGN ONLY ENDS ONE WAY (WITH IGN)
BAD ENDINGS
TO SALVE THE FEET OF THE MIND
POT PLANTS AND CANDLES UNTIL
LIGHT AT THE END OF THE TERROR
OF EVERYTHING THAT IS EVERYTHING
MEANS MECHANICAL MYSTICISM
AS AN ARCHITECTURE OF HUNTS
DISGUISED AS A HOMING PIGEON
ANYTHING BUT ITSELF.

'sniffing glue instead of your masonic brandies'

watch your tongue crawl up the spiral staircase \ relax / of course you won't / own a spiral staircase / in fact \ this story starts where all good stories start / meet me at the thin place with rizla, mugwort / we're going back to the birthplace of homosexuality \ keep me hanging at the temple gates / hi butterfly of history, I am caterpillar fetish \ skinning a raw bear / going to sleep together / Burnt civilisation is a stove \ bear burritos / garlic \ onion \ ginger / wrong order/ the dread inherent is reassurance / i'm sure it will taste fine/ we speak in undercooked tongues / the communal living minded poltergeist does our dishes \ my physical form is the burned-over district, new york state / too many cults in me already my eyes some kind of shaker / hands holy roller / skin seance / no more utopian social movements below this hairline / fracture all the religions i archaeologied already \ all the archaeologies s i religioned already/ high density of UFOs in certain areas / nothing paranormal, it's a celestial garage / they feed everyone baked goods \ like bread / really honestly / nobody with a gluten intolerance has ever been abducted by aliens and lived to tell the tale \ there we go again \ falling through into the next world fair \ caught between materialism and a non-place \ saw something i could perceive / as the constellation taurus \ which could have been the constellation taurus / who cares \ at this point every word is a metaphor for who knows \ no longer cinnamon scented scars but scars scented cinnamon / i call it the natural order and \ nobody can stop me / eating sugar cubes with my foraged nettle soup \ and still declaring this a fucking disaster all the same \ there's something more out there in the universe it's not just us which is good because i really hate / work \

FULL MOON LEECH PARTY

what is going on and why is it eating everything - ·
are you succulent, pig?
i snarl-want geodesic dome austerity,
the austerity of sacred geometry, fear
of the seeping night, fucking up upwards, another
finger. not this austerity
of domesticity's sandwich spread
bright dull markt salmon, literally dead but
worse still - actually dead. I tear off my top layer of skin
to practice tanning animal hides so I can make myself
a winter jacket myself out of myself
fuck u capitalism, who's laughing now? me
because i can build a fire to roast chestnuts
and warm my hands
but you
don't even have hands.
people are not made of bricks, they're mostly made of systems, my drag
persona is called Nature.
luckily there is no crime anymore then
but for now i spend my time under
ground searching for the early warning signs
of sinkholes i might cover in green ribbons, moss and build
homes inside like everyone's arms that have ever been
a small architecture of warm blood
i am wearing a terror halo that burns when i feel
fear, so we can find each other glowing in the tunnels
there's no curse to cast, just a protection charm
PROTECTION AND ALL THAT IT IMPLIES
if it implies what it could imply, well.

my eyeballs are so heavy in their
sockets, they're in my throat and i can't swallow / come
closer and read me your truth movement, i can lick your turmeric
stains, grimoire or
stick some parts of some concepts to my skin like leeches
i hate the ideology of the belief of the system of
bricks of people who declare that
bloodletting has no proven medicinal benefit
but now i am sitting in a bath covered in feasting leeches
and i don't even have the words
to thank them for their labour

A Cloud Based Infrastructure For Caloric Intake Estimation From Pre Meal Videos And Post Meal Plate Waste

i am such an embittered attempt at a plaster ceiling, i'm infinite
space in deep space and our concentrated capacity
for endless compassion but
i wanted to be a ceiling
or at least a rafter

they're getting closer, the sub-government that is, i can feel it
spinning the room the milkweed on the horizon is not
foreboding always a clue in and of itself?
drywall adjective heavy beam of left
behind terror tempered bricks

the omniverse's drunk without us or any invitation to us
stayed up all night to get lucky, to watch
the Kennedy assassination - nothing better
to do than nothing - the speaker shouts silently:
unschool the pentagon

what is the left behind and able to
be lenient about a part from this decorative
server farm i have painted dazzle
camouflage the joke is jagged catastrophe teased online
banking passwords from The Book of the Law

manuscripts on how to name lack
of ambition under this system, piggybacking death
because the human body is not safe for work
i am 1/4 illuminati but only on my father's side so it doesn't
really count — i get very little responsibility, just this really

low level mysticism spells oblivion backwards
synchronised swimming crystals don't
call it a stream of consciousness don't
anthropomorphise fate it will do it itself thanks
there's more over fish in the ocean, for now coddle certainty

tamper berry fall down the spiral, torrent theory beneath
the conspiracy theorised technically is the conspiracy
theorised as neck hair 'plausible' is cause for concern

i don't believe your magic-seed i'm sorry
but i do love a good christmas tree decoration to effigy a police
with i do feel the warmth of picking ticks from each other
after a day by the river

the only reason i was abducted by aliens in kathmandu in 1994 was that in 1994 i went to kathmandu to be abducted by aliens

and to try and feel the difference between this state of being
and another turn on the simulation that the world is not
rugged earth-worm miner, it is all a broken chemistry set
wave the earth bye from the car window, cough up kisses
the spreadsheet of the fabric of the space time continuum
sorry that it wasn't a freudian slip, i love it enough really

he who does not work
neither
shall
he
eat.
destroy work and eat everything

hallelujah i'm an acultural producer of mythologies, unable
to digest the latent ones, hallelujah i'm a sea monkey in
the vague puddle of existence and you are also a sea monkey
in the vague puddle of existence and i think you are cute
for what it's worth to a brine shrimp, all crustaceans are
beautiful! dear world affairs: how DARE you make me feel

like punk is relevant again, this is so embarrassing for all
i thought we lived in a post-Police Pagan Association world
still life with roses, sauerkraut and lost digital tax return
how much wild chamomile must i pick to pay off my student
loan, at least in the eyes of god? it's so cold i can't see my
hands despite the politics of care i attempt to uphold wept

swindle and dualistic opposition to dualism, the future is
larvae to birth the past of itself haunted by a dream of the
world as a shining silver globe dripping with disinfectant
topped with a raw tied up joint of meat sitting like what
is left to do but haunt you with the promise of maggots
and a future for your species? Nine worlds is not enough,

recruit, recruit, recruit! i WISH that the queen was a lizard
wyrd shelters wyrd bold cutters wyrd warmth wyrd superglue
there is no repetition only multiple invocations of spirit
this escalation that keeps escalating, remember when the
world ended that single time? minuscule bonfire against the

flood dreams i despised the consensus until it left and some

of us were still left out here doing the work of mild psychosis
the word of milk psychosis, trying to find new ways to tie
our shoelaces. ice caps ice caps ice caps forgot to refill the tray
after that last whisky, oh well going to have to slur whatever
narrative is needed next i hope it has dragons because i tried
to assimilate you see, but then my hands turned to ectoplasm

Semi- Homemade

I'm no less real than Australia
          and to be
          actual total what
                    are the symptoms of appendix

sought out this state of slapdash
                         microcosm which is merely all
     knowing but unsure how
          to successively acknowledge the uninterrupted

stream of symptoms upon symptoms limping
up mud in the throat this escalating lifestyle
we bombard the significant with our
          bloody sweat fears

ramparts of the farmers market nevertheless
arguable the extent to which a white
male body is a Body in the traditional
sense a friendly quasi body explains wealth

               management companies already own
     the land that will be the coast feeling
like pickled banded together bright tangerine musk built polis
          city of the antiquity romantic beaming un-

food bank un un necessary mortality rates
     no fake farm names to stave off competition from farm farms
farm farms in their intrinsically inferior reality
                    this is our last BIG FUN ROCKET SHIP CENTURY

New Zealand Silicon Valley Apocalypse Bunker Prep Century
not a fucking harvest festival
          keep up
          sheep off the big table

i plait my hair w/ cabbage leaves
               lean against cracked stones
the good thing about the cockroach team is even if
    you lose

you win in the long spore

nihilist mattress purchase november

I could cook all the best for you in the Iron Age fort I have
constructed around my brain and ankles but also the present
incidental That extended navy empiring dusk punctuated
by a crop circle within a crop circle punctured
by a badly carved lightning stain punctuated
by my dissection of the landscape as puncturable
subject Among the salted snow the salted snails

the snowdrops spring melt so (fuck nature, tenderly
the sledding slope the salted sledding utopic
things and more over things that are considered
hyper improbable to occur are most often considered
lucky to occur, which was once true/*ish* or another possible never,
friendly unkind diesel motor spirit - i promise to spite
to craft you a most beautiful carbon neutral coffin

There's nothing that could not happen so of course
it *is* fucking terrifying, a genre of rational sink
Crystalline metabolism wailing impossible hallucination
in which I am full of labradorite shards embellishing
more magnificent creature comforts septic hygienic cultural spheres
To be a successful prophet margin one must honour good
marketing experience, hawk the most prevalent

archetypal desired fears of a? self-referential ghost
population whilst avoiding becoming reduced
to idiosyncratic marmalade or piracy fault lines,
the hubris tariff (*lol-guffaw at cultural permanence in the spirit
realm* A gleaming and scooped-out jury that has already decided
that that is that Favourite fate-late capitulation Unsettling
marathon running towards a theory of cliffs

Which side are n't you on? My stomach
hurts so I know this is n't my place You're *gay*? But
then who's the *cause* and who's the *effect*?? TRIPLE
FRYING EVERYTHING NO PENSION! the way the dusk
reflects off Blairite glass onto the sparkling faces of people
I sense dislike around - hate it 's fine - compassion it 's fine -
Drawing fractal spirals to circle navigate the market

context despite despising exploitable fluidity -

probably it 's not fine. *LEAVE HISTORY ALONE.*
A sickly p;ink haze emanating spores
from the country's decomposing innards, directed panspermia
as seen from a European budget bird's eye's view
Neatly compartmentalised abjection of agriculture fading
softly into the abyss, the Hot desk at the satanic mills

The last ever Christmas bonus Libidinal standing stone
circles and virginal rocks and British jobs for the crisis
of us British workers Young Britons could become food-
What is edible given the right? some foodstuffs:
ZERO HOURS AND WEETABIX AND THE JAM
-BASED ECONOMY AND C.B.T. AND MILTON
KEYNES REALLY FUCKING SERIOUSLY

MILTON KEYNES BUT EQUALLY
COSMOPOLITAN MERINGUE FATIGUE
I Could build you 500,000 forest dens to compensate
for your country's lack of welfare state
Rugged communitarianism handsome reactionary
plaid shirt Temporary hunger Fun!!
i could steal you enough brassicas

to feed a crimethinc novel
Dark chocolate and the enviable self-delusion of evasion
but also it's sort of the end of the world, you can stop pretending
you don't like milk chocolate
Scavenged myself sort of soft and hard grow
new power tools, new limbs at the molten core
Something was salvaged, not very finely chopped dust light

Flaming crushed lighthouse beckoning
Tree sap ejaculate on the second horizon
Memorial mugs for the Mars bombing
Invisible oppositional defiance disorder
Extra extra butter from our imaginary cow
named after a French philosopher feasting on the daisies
in translation of the imaginal field work tripped depression tap

tap tapping the wire in time with the terror watch
Dog lost-internet wept at the Jarman School of Conservatism,
blocked and clocked England ketamine architecture crusty dub
reggae party absolute arrest and totalling failure on every axis
measurable My hope for a future starts hanging out with the ones

who've thrown a past at me on the street - bye - whatever - plenty more
hopes to be had Fixed the game skywards, towards hell and mushrooms

if i scrawl on myself *EARTHLING* will i live long enough
that that becomes a weird planetary-nationalist
identity Will? what At this moment
I'm just struggling to sleep with myself
but I'm fine enough, I'm the poet laureate
of this lentil stew! for the physical 1% of all matter, pagan and pagan
and pray for who wants a shit accomplice? enchanting

terror turmeric blanket hug the comfort of the yuga narrative
yeah I'm reading dead people for faith again
it's helping my back pain to be reminded
of the honour of a back that can feel pain
and still bend over backwards to conclude:
no *we* cannot see the stars tonight, clouds
staying tender to the incomprehensible

my self esteem is all fucked up
there's oat milk in my porridge
and i might not make you cum
but i can always precisely
chop an onion very slowly

somehow you love me

now it's the commons and we all
borrow each other's shoes i am
opulent in my wealth of ill fitting
rain boots running my fingers
through a thousand intricate laces

I like scaffolding as much as the next attempt to create order

what are all those things that have apparently happened
          somewhere? the repetitive strain injuries of history -
to demonstrate on a personal and political level can someone
or you show me the way to my pre-historic bones? I am yet somehow
enough full of beer and your carpal bones on the back of some
of my skull tender in public that hate crime is an almost
imperceptible shimmer on the horizon of this u-bahn station,
I estimate that feeling is at least a vertebrae or purple clavicle,
so i give thanks to the tongue of the dawn choir. chaotic
good burns the streets, chaotic
neutral stains the sheets, it's not not reverent
it's a feeling refracted
fuck shit up
            politic of snuck, dialectical glamour,
sideways glimmers at the sideways
          glances shiny plastic chandelier branches -
fuck heterosexuality's matt
      gloss, municipal pheromones cut with talc -
here everything is tilted tit for gilded tat;
decorate the use away, etch sweat and melt into the crisis of feeling's
brittle solution: a minor gateau, i stopped being afraid of aviation
catastrophe and now use my time in the air to jump at the sun,
assess my place on the Beck suicide ideation scale, address
the state of my nation's blood circulation - my praxis
is *camp* hatred i.e. i do not want to make anything
that would not make people think
        I would not work with the Zabludowicz,
i swear and it's the funnest option, the real champagne is always
claiming ecstatic agency in this vacuum
that we're all just trying to sleep sitting up in
a comfy yet stylish eyemask, none work with left pleasure.
the chronic mental health thing which affects [insert multiple objects]
          is, like a letter from the state, apparently
not who i am, which is lucky but discouraging
journey work - back to the drawing board to scrub the cave
                        wall clean of fortune's misplaced fire again,
dye a flag night
                with the charcoal from my burnt down spare rib
But i am partially what I am, among other fallacies: contemporary
artist on budget flight between european countries, 20-
something pragma-gendered animal sad about accidents of

spilt hormones and adrenaline junkyard chemical contamination
communist poet doubting the politics of that distinctly
worn opulence but still blaming the moon, i avoid anything
that scares me out in the great unwild so i can subject myself
to it under laboratory conditions, bandage the fag
ash under my skin on my own terms,
science can be fun and holy blood fiction,
experimental collectivised endorphins, it's funny
how even these small baroque unpleasures could be ripped away,
used against me, against me like my funny use of funny,
queer, impending harsh irony and nothing taken
            for granted under current climate
conditional lenses fucked against the stained glass of the public
sphere, give me irreverence or give me death
or both whatever i don't care which, i just really care
for obnoxious joy, hyacinths dainty by the hearth
        sometimes I am asked who the work is for
and the answer is it is for nobody having to work but
some days, like tonight, the answer is just if you know you
know you don't have to lie to me, i know
you're telling the truth, subterfuge
      evades everything these days via
the opacity of everything all at once sober
libations to this silly thing i call a self flitting
disposable during the light
touch approach to life
found after declining
demented hops and the strobe of public life
repeatedly in favour of imaginary honeysuckle woven
a sunshade against the indigestion of iridescent light fixtures
i have no soluble solution i'm just learning to slice
            the garlic thinner with age
give my real name to the state
as my monastic name, lying
to be true to save my
soul's head (the
soul's soul has no sense
of bureaucracy and therefore is
                        in no danger)
i am pure dark light and gently fried
rainbow chard, sesame oil, warm almond milk
accepting the risk that articulation is the problem
but i love it, so here is a model i built of it collapsing
some sub adequate recovery process, leaked formula

the escape plan looks impossible in this font so i'm planning
to rewrite it in perfect cursive in gilded invisible ink
then i will burn it to cook the best roast potatoes
see let it never be said i disregard materiality
the price of oil shoulders or multiple fingers
i fill the keyboard with all my leftover skin shit,
same as the next hoarder of sentient excess
some just trade it all in for gold
                just like that all gone
in the blink of an eye the world vanishes
and reappears and vanishes and reappears
so many times every minute
and yet i am still so scared every single time
don't fucking stop

If you think pigeons are too common to be beautiful don't call yourself a communist

The dogs in Picassos!
The happiest protagonists in anything anywhere!
walked around looking at the dogs
and thinking about
you + sunshine all the time
a distant psy-trance party
this bedroom entirely removed from
the economics that enable it

I am a Picasso dog
Picasso was a misogynist
but it's okay, dogs have no gender
Run around like a puppy
at the bottom of a painting who
never even had to learn
the meaning of Modernism
The slobbering ecstasy of now
is enough to be getting on with
(no Futurism)

For all I know that dog is a cat
Blame the politics of abstraction
not me but it doesn't matter
it's the number of legs that count

My ears prick up to
palm tree the heart against
the sky
Talking to everybody
the forehead opens to
breaking grinning
pour out a coke for O'Hara
Capital has to die inasmuch
as it is an inadequate model
for understanding desire

my head is falling off
for you
behead the bourgeoisie
manic episode

sandcastle of duvets
                no need for poems now
running back into the burning house
to rescue our cat-dog

Untitled (for axle)

regardless of subjective 'badness'
the apple never falls far from the womb of the thought
okay so my biology is less than great, a
lost letter bloody placenta apple tree of species bounda
but who is to say that greatness or discretion
was not always problem or at least
problem's lost bodyguard? can discretion be to discretion
as
discrete is to discreet? because i meant discretion
a spare body Calmed by the scale of the roadsign:

TEMPELHOF
HAMBURG
SATURN

a reminder that everywhere that is not where you are is equally
far away as the crow flies because the crow is doing his own thing
and does not exist to define you in relation to the road
systems you attempt to temporally position your life
movements within. as a friend:
the most direct route is an empty canal upholstered
with carnivorous plants and the
smell of boiled jasmine
because we drank all the bathwater
and ate all the lilies
inhaled all the vapour of the past and now
high below sea level
this present is inaccessible moisture ice break
brick work binge
like the year we all took plant fertiliser and became beautiful
plants
thriving
paranoid indoor office ferns with nosebleeds running
snot libraries melded birdsong and a motorway
is my shit for sure. celestial service station
telepathic to the exhaust fumes
earnest splinter group on the edge of the industrial lunatic fringe
camp punk garden shed veranda potluck sunset culture war
texts at right angles to
the landscape's disappearing insights
the production of a lifestyle

what is prosperity if not internalised
rubber bricks, fake yolk, hollow pastry?
the privilege of at least having the pastry
the means to imagine interior fruits
my therapist compliments my 'powerful words' and sentence structure
i say yeah i already know about
that problem

•

national flags all promote pride in the same great nation,
the great nation of flag.   fuck that, let's spit in each others
faces   in the dark and
call it the great nation of
too obvious rhyming joke
calling the muses to come
a sidetone on muses: in my reading when sappho
says 'muse' it means something like 'poetry ghost'
which is to say the muse is not the object or the
subject but the facilitation or maybe praxis
which is to say people are not muses they are
discrete people at their own discretion but the muse is the
motorway or fiberoptic cable or pavement between our
houses or air between our faces that enables the spirit flow
calling the muses to come
and pat me on the shoulder   and tell me it will be okay but
reassurance is not their job   and i understand
so i sit on my own with them
observing the homoerotics of breathing
the same exact number of exhaust fume chemicals
as you are breathing now on a separate continent
bunking the u-bahn again bc i refuse to pay for muses
and anyway today i am empty to poetry bc i am waiting
for you to reply to my email about croci
in the graveyard between our houses
so the entire affective potential of the english language
(plus our token schlecht deutsch affectations)
is in your hands and nervous system
and as with the muses, i know this
is not in the job description
so i will sit by this canal and not wait
but do other things instead.
it might sound like i love you
but don't worry, i don't yet,
i just have my moon in lion mane and there's an

impending new moon
and the old and new world orders are collapsing
into one solid disk in the sky and i try to shield myself
from its complex system of weights pulleys and grammars
but the oblique point is the terrifying realisation i could love you
in this landscape or even whichever happens next.

A BLACKBERRY SMEARED AGAINST YOUR CHEEK AGAINST THE GOVERNMENT

MY LEFT ARMPIT ACHES FROM BEING BITTEN
THERE'S NO METAPHOR IT'S JUST GAY SEX
INASMUCH AS THOSE THINGS ARE DIVISIBLE
PAST X VALUE FORMING IN ABUNDANT EXCESS
NOBODY needs TO WASTE ANY WORDS OR SWEAT
FLUID FAG GERANIUM LIQUIDISED NEW MOON
CHAMPAGNE AMARETTO ARMPIT HAIR IN TEETH
WILL YOU LOVE MY MASC VENUS OPULENCE
THE WAY I WILL BATHE FOR HOURS
ADD MORE HOT WATER FOREVER UNTIL
I CHANGE BACK INTO THE SAME STAINED WHITE
T-SHIRT I'VE BEEN WEARING SINCE YOU LAST SAW ME?
TOO EARLY TO SAY BUT MEAN WHILE IN THE SOFT TIME
LET'S STRIVE FOR THIS LEVEL OF LUXURY IN EVERYTHING
REVOLVED LEFTWARDS VELVET TEETH MARKING THE
FOPPISH TILT OF THE DOMESTIC AXIS GAILY ROUTINE
CHUCKLED PINK HIMALAYAN SALT OVER SPILT WINE

IN THE REAL WORLD I TYPE THE WORD 'MARX' FOR MONEY
TO BUY US ALL THESE DIFFERENT POTATOES HONEY
SUGAR AGAVE DARLING ORIGAMI MODELS OF THE PASTORAL
UTOPIA I USE AS AN UNDERSTUDY FOR NEVER TYPING 'MARX'
AGAIN THE DIALECTICS OF MY SHOULDER PAIN AND YOURS
I BELIEVE IN COLLECTIVITY BECAUSE IT IS IMPOSSIBLE
TO ADEQUATELY BITE YOUR OWN ARMPIT LUCKILY
I DON'T need TO PAY RENT BECAUSE I THREW ALL MY COINS
INTO A BEAUTIFUL18TH CENTURY GREEN BRONZE
WATER FEATURE FOR LUCK FROM THE GODS
REASSURE ME ABOUT MY FINANCIAL DECISIONS OR
NIBBLE MY EAR UNTIL THEY DON'T EXIST OR WE CAN
LIE IN BED AND WAIT BECAUSE FUCK THE INSTRUCTIVE FORM
ONE DAY THE SMELL OF MY SWEAT WILL REMIND ME
MORE OF YOU THAN ME AND I PROMISE TO CHERISH
THAT HOWEVER LONG IT LASTS LET'S FEED EACH OTHER
FROM THE MUSK OF THE WET EARTH AND ARMPITS
METICULOUSLY SPILT CORNUCOPIA OF GRENADINE
LAND OF PLENTY SPONTANEOUS ADORATION
FROLICKING IN THE NEW MEADOWS
ABSENCE OF POLLEN ALLERGIES
AFTER THE REVOLUTION
THE GRATIN DAUPHINOIS

ABOLISHED IN ASHES IN THE HEARTH

The pressure of productivity has nothing to offer
is the mantra to be repeated at leisure
here are some of my many rose-scented wrists
the curvature of the holy grail dispersed in hermetic space-time
throwing a little glitter on the universe's single atom
a plug to stop the sinking stomach dragging the body
to the floor but into the soil of ancient disgust for ancient
lies bruised ideology of the queer pastoral fingering the idyll making
peace with our ticks as accumulated knowledge of someone
else's means of reproduction outside our own inside bodies
marginal lichen sinking into the husk of the purple ocean fantasy
of unclaimable internal space for the starfish militias
holding in my palm a caterpillar the exact same value
as myself feather and rock fall at the same speed forever
across a lowland of theorisation abruptly chopped
into the nettle soup of the place behind our wisdom
teeth where diminishing language comes from and lays
to rest the very notion of a legible subject but
simply left-leaning smile and infinity loop held
together by the flesh of our teeth, ribbons, spring
dandelions, the threat of poisonous snakes still writhing
below the ontologically arrogant surface certainty
of a white bone china European subjecthood
transformation requires a worshipping of the maggots
who will build gondolas from their spit
and carry me and my endearing melodrama
to the billions of mulch afterlives that await us all
I think it's really beautiful when people get eaten
by their pets after death
our bodies can grow roses or feed really cute dogs
the mountain eats the orange pink sun
the terrestrial sphere has it all figured out
taking the world slowly and at face value
there are no dots to be connected
there is a single dot
tinny panpipe music and pagan ritual at regional conference centre
the sprawling Tempest producing the universal adamant
that the world can get better become displaced into
its own arms all forgiven a magnanimous spring
blossom warm and cosy hot chocolate from the
dandelion root of the problem banning bloodsports

taking spare risks for later banishing the soap suds
from under our eyelids letting go of the notion
that there is a single verb who can save us
I keep grasping the nettle I keep fucking it up
It keeps hurting life is beautiful fucking non-linearity
split ends multiple organism a gnostic approach
to traversing the barren planes somewhere the
nest lit by continuous fires since the spring dawn
of time reserves a place for you with mammoth
meat and vegan marshmallows and we
smile at the fire, grateful to have finally
stopped transcending our own survival
temporally elsewhere a brittle worm
between teeth crawls into the market
to die as a delicate new delicacy
I keep leaving my head places to do my research
on the best ways to escape from quicksand
whilst my body gets indifferently eaten
by saber-toothed tigers to grasp
at the end of the spiral whirlpool drenched
soggy elegant grass stained back
time in the time of time
I feed the animals
from the palm
of my lung

A CHEMTRAIL IN CURVED AIR

and who will really be laughing
when diamanté gloves are off and all
sweaty teeth have come out
so we are the godhead's laughing
gums joyful bleeding
whatever bloody oil mud pie chart is the world leaking common
sense and even heading nearer to absolute
done and joker and spiralling underneath
cracked dead meal replacement
matter's neglected spirograph

i enter the next turning of my subculture with
my head held high mighty
nd born again stone-washed meritocracy

pragmatic architecture drips down some
throats but the ghostly orbits all
is not
lost without a solid latex glove nd commitment to the company
norm no strange new old time burial practices
can actually do the celestial cleansing intacting
sterilising proud ID deed or enforce rejoining the herd

despite this found naked yet again nd made weird nd
new in a field of poppies nd male
nd female humans
so deemed too wild too cow mutilation
to be a real man or real major threat
cryotherapist wet healing closer to rapid
fire question win-a-fridge-freezer
rounds in before citizenship to the scrapings
of the sandy arctic
melt bomb hung sky to relative antiseptic

a thousand constellations held in a single double stomach
romantic service station burger king
the wormhole could be anywhere as marx
said 'i know it's boring
but sometimes we have to do things
that are boring
it will give you more opportunities at the end of history'

among melted down breeze block crystals the reconstructed
druid lazy iron age
rainbow tie dye aesthetic questions summons some dainty iced
victoria sandwich demons it's a challenge and i
love this fucking muster
ready for anything action spirits
always use the back door double wink
a case in point this rose quartz lube chandelier this
vision of stone henge as a fluid stained weighted blanket

ecstatic unfurnished domestic
mind palace wallpapered in infinite
bronze sculpture forget-me-not-notes
screaming out to breath slower you
ungrateful bonobo go do a new sex thing
feel sunset melting off your battle scabs
to their golden pus laden marrow

Terence McKenna Psy-Trance Sample sample

i may be getting more conservative with age as you can smell
i have come to love the scent of a municipal water feature
reaping the rewards of all my new labours
rejoicing in the knowledge a pelvic muscle group could break
my raised fist and yet
that doesn't mean the scathing sell-out smirk
doesn't emanate inward expelling
a million millions of dead cops badges
lost prairie fire dog pups edward abbey capybara bath video gala

finding refuge in unflinching complicity knot-working but the
unreality of
the situation sneaks up n bites me back down into an earlier bardo
of awareness of this building as it continues going cult
documentaries about cults down with the mundane
might of the empire snaking world and so what
if the banner doesn't fit on a banner
all out lavender bathtub poppers on the empty streets

elsewhere caught between posterity and my own
preemption and space rocks and a non-place
prime location for this 6.30am sharp obituary party
mildly concerned about
wasting the free wine of
the mind in a go-slow strike against
everything it has to offer by offering it a comradely
13 hours of Terence McKenna against the instant recuperation
of its natural unspoilt resources

in the tradition of the western esoteric tradition please
can i experience something i haven't
been taught to think i know how to understand to relieve
some of my minor bourgeois affiliations
false flag crisis actor of my own melodrama pour a thousand
hours of speculative bullshit into this pristine mountain stream

found the next article to count backwards from
all these death dates to embalm and empower
my sinkhole anxiety further spiralling
past the NASA guards
to fall off the cliffs at the edge

of Antarctica strobed to comforting void sleep
the confederacy of mushrooms hides aliens within lizard's secret
organisations to mask the real capitalism which is bigfoot running
the catholic church on our flat earth hiring shapeshifters to pick fights with
civilians and weapons caches still consult nazis especially with regards to
russians, mass shootings, teflon pans and the media used to be
the united kingdom under the hollow earth and the real
wall street and they are mushrooms
and they are
you are me are
                                        everything are one with the universe are
                                              finally relief from all these consciousness

No Songs

i play yahtzee w my sad dad
        wounded masc country
sung until i don't even care to notice
            when i throw
                                    yahtzee

it's a genre defined by harvesting un or anti wellness as metaphysical
      gelatinous abundance i protest
   it casts itself out to see! anew good and trve metal for life jackets
      stored under the soil insolence!
      biodiversity!
      like that other decade w the floating baby
a reusable canvas angst
if you will

big a little a fermented b
the system might have got u
and it might get m/e

so not to be overly technical or whether
but whether punk
      can or cannot be
dead is a question
   of agency of sentience of
ideas in this century and a few preceding meaning: meaning:

the woodsmoke 3D printer is working
          but right now?
with all these demographically severed heads rolling around
                    the ship's parlour staining the tea strainer
                    camouflage blood?
you call it nature one more time and i swear i will
you
don't dare take advantage of my home
          -made 'i don't call the police except
                              never' disco ball
the sphincter in the mirror clenched holding the mind
              of whatever reason i wanted
              yesterday is called to reason over eggs and amyls

over easy equanimous riot porn channel

hopping too reason from the easy spot
it's all meek fun because auditing threats will have their way
with everyone
even the hardest core pinnacle of humanity all happened
yesterday which is what i call everyday
in this post-enlightment materialist void of a slumped
soggy k-hole
i for one also find
the anti social movements of my
hands very interesting
pure electrocuted meat food for the soul-brain
punk's not dead because s/he always was
everything is
a system
it's hard
to see
from the liver

[submariner] the mid horizon opens fleeting down butterflies
magenta faced fossil men on horses to kill the stock
exchange continues merrily brutally towards our collective
red burning end face whatever the olden time
folds slipping through the last spring fog is still
a unit sometimes to swap for food or shelter beneath
golden tresses of auburn hope abandoned chalk
on the pavement when the road is blocked the road
is blocked and that is a dialectical fact pointing to our lack
of imagination as still conceptualising it as a road the real
reason was always beyond explanation because that's what nature
is nature is whatever is unacceptable as unacceptable things
learnt from hurling mercury and staking out each other
with planks of silver to practice for what is promised from the life
we have learnt by virtue of the way things have been bridled
together haphazard under the hood is expectantly a sculpture
boulevard of carefully disintegrated monuments refracted
so whatever is the feeling that can't be sunk death is a social
contract yes real but equally not or simultaneously everywhere
on the fortean spectrum of reality to unreality that's the thing
that truth loves to beckon in doomed mammal expeditions
letting fake go of making petroleum sense time leaks among

the hot feather wine the secondary sex characteristics dance
but echo leads meta brass cock ring the elephant in
in the machine soft bundle of history but what a cute
girl i mean boy oh my god i'm so sorry what a brave boy
to have withstood that she's so sweet there really was never
a battlement anyhow or more than can be spoken of as rough
equivalence to the vegan chocolate in the advent calendar
at the end of this world also a socially outsourced dissolved
ice refreshing burning flood plains whispering invincible
essence the deep core of essentially okay is all the the is really
some people call it a self but magnolia tree i state
just another missive from the transsexual demons

Transitional Demands

and so we meet in a middle plateau of warped crass
embroidery
patched khaki so beholden to my hallucination
where no one is police
except of course the cops who cannot be real flesh n blood n
un intended consequences
this trip hazard unfortunately breeds a million new cop
possession incidents an infectious epidemic

even snapping mutual ankles to buckwheat
flour out in the faked real shared
baking vegan felt i was always neatly icing the target
on the periphery
like revolving the fucked intricacies of what we could
make cinnamon you
get me you know by the way the
evening twilight hits the database
results an abstraction of the full blood count of the rusty
cut up nation state
the thing about the war is that it is a war and government is war

and even here we find that way that is a bramble
-induced laugh through welp
surprised to find a we that is a black bloc sound system
sticker covered two way mirror
so what if i was just in it for a countercultural parent-y figure
needed a window smashed to vision many intolerable things
are tolerable it turns out later is the tragedy of it all
lukewarm milky surrender punk upholstery
the bittersweet kettle i needed for this nettle tea

is we all have had our addiction issues and yet
everyone has their own history with everything
i might just be a angry trans pup player still angry about
when i was 7 aka the 28th G8 summit so a conclusion to start
maybe it is both as some say a neoliberal project and necessary
to pay a surgeon to cut my chest open, so for now but i'll keep wishing
i had a friend to do it for me with some dental floss and a bottle of spirits

Human Fruit Machine

In the age before the baby drew any sum
of the Bible from the fleeting
warmth of the sun

That's not where we are now, though

We are when the decisions about basic existence
or after will come
on pale mint paper and passive moderate disgust

Some of my gender is inevitably what I have been
handed to dry my eyes whilst crying at medical professionals
re-articulated:
however much hair I grow wherever, I remain hysteria-adjacent
even if your voice is less of a fireworks
hair distribution is simply the difference
between naturalised feminine distress and stagy faggy melodrama

either way, fuck off back to the opera, maria callas

Why are you crying?

Most likely explanation: weird interspecies sex
And millions of years later
Here I am
Resentful primo donno
Filling in a checklist

Bodily autonomy has a special quality of being
retro-actively deletable, as soon as you don't
have it, you never did

The limit is stainless steel and polite and hand sanitiser and not liable

I plead, my canon! My elegant canon is hopelessly irretrievably
mundane male and basically disgusting men, grasping for essentialism
Look at this beautiful acne and arrogance and abject
Bersanian glamour and hell tell me what's up in my
blood right this very year?

Can't imagine not at least imagining

crushing on my gender therapist my meditation teacher
if only for the illicit love of a structure to hate
a rigid immovable force to push
up against like a sex
or personality

I used to think they existed and now
I don't which is the only way
it gets better

Trying to see God is like trying to hold
your own hand or be the poppers
and the blood vessels

Was it worth it to Maria Callas?

Ferocious Lack Harmony

when we picture the end of the world i hope
we can find it adorned with rose blossom and
a million bonfires of dead cops as literal as you like
a fountain spilling the cracks in the foundation
alluding to an absence of base of superstructure you
know the thing i mean i hope when we picture the
end of the world is an opulent credits sequence without
names my primary metaphor for the death of ego is
dumpling stew we can all be dumplings darling it will
be warm and undistinguished a haphazard orgy of
slightly better weather than we currently experience
simply through our altered perceptions of better a
magnificent collapsible spittle diamond against progress the
new cum will taste so good as good even as the old cum
our rapidly expanding human animal consciousness
ricocheting of the walls of the space time continuum
an infinite percentage of that also containing the
redundancy of digital marketing executives it is
going to be so beautiful i hope when we picture the
end of the world fire feels hotter yeah we want it all fucking
gross and fucking twee up against the wall motherfucker
remember men me neither i might have even been one imagine
the end of the world the abolition of egg white omelettes
nothing less than fully bucolic bourgeois hobbit utopia
tropical islands gay ramblers association of the mind
at a leisurely breast stroke pace i'm regressing again
but all i hope is when we picture the end of the world
we end the picture of the world

NOVELTY THEORY is the term Terrance McKenna used to describe his theory, based on study of fractals and the I Ching, of moments in time ebbing and flowing between novelty and habit.

Untitled (A Farewell to Progress)

Buckminster Fuller - *Operating Manual for Spaceship Earth*

Wingnut Dishwasher's Union - *Jesus Does The Dishes*

Cornelius Cardew - *Revolution is the Main Trend*

John Barker - *'In 1971-72, I was convicted in the Angry Brigade trial and spent seven years in jail. In my case, the police framed a guilty man.'*

Lochi - *London Acid City*

Blondie - *Heart of Glass*

Minutemen - *History Lesson Pt. II*

Iain Spence - *The Sekhmet Hypothesis*

Magnus Ljunggren - *Poetry and Psychiatry: Essays on Early Twentieth-Century Russian Symbolist Culture*

THEY NO VISION SAW
(For Phil Ochs and Paul Bennewitz)

Title is from *The Diggers Song*

they have no evidence that asylum Europeans or Eastern seekers are responsible for reported reductions in the swan population

Title is an alteration of a refused request for a correction in The Sun newspaper, *'The story was based on unsubstantiated allegations made by unnamed members of the public who claimed to believe that swans were being killed and eaten by Eastern Europeans. The police have confirmed that nobody has been arrested for such offences, and they have no evidence that asylum-seekers or Eastern Europeans are responsible for reported reductions in the swan population.'* More information available at MediaWise.org.uk

John Zerzan - *Elements of Refusal*

¡TchKung! - *Smash Things Up*

Wolves in the Throne Room

BATHS SUCK BUT THE STATE DOESN'T

Title comes from a San Francisco gay anarchist pamphlet that I have lost to the depths of the internet/archive, so I acknowledge a debt to queer ancestors past but unfortunately can't be more specific.

Françoise d'Eaubonne - Speech at General Assembly of FHAR (front homosexuel d'action révolutionnaire)

The Head is a Headless Hunter

Jon Kabat-Zinn - *Full Catastrophe Living*

another empty threat to disappear

Bruce LaBruce - *The Revolution is My Boyfriend*

Defiance County, Ohio

Defiance, Ohio

The Diggers Song

CRASS - *Fight War Not Wars*

according to wikipedia i am in the 'initial struggle for success' phase of my life as bruce springsteen's life

The title, transparently, comes from Bruce Springsteen's Wikipedia page

Good Luck - *Stars Were Exploding*

TRAVEL DIARY SUMMER 2016

Independent (Online), Tuesday 9 July 2013 - *'British public wrong about nearly everything, survey shows'*

Better Than Sex (For Simon Chapman)

Martha Rosler - *Semiotics of the Kitchen*

the reverse of a ramification is buttered toast

Fanny Paul Clinton - *'I am not at all ambitious, if it was up to me all i would do is read novels and fuck.'*

A pause to glare at the person next to me in the cafe who just laughed whilst saying 'failed utopia'

Lucy Parsons - *'We must devastate the avenues where the wealthy live.'*

Theses on Land Masses (After Ian Hamilton Finlay)

Andy Warhol - *'land really is the best art'*

The Wicker Man (1973)

The Eel in the Sink

Semi-Homemade

Title is from TV chef Sandra Lee's cooking concept.

'sniffing glue instead of your masonic brandies'

Title from Derek Jarman's *The Last of England.*

FULL MOON LEECH PARTY

CRASS - *Big A, Little A*

A Cloud Based Infrastructure For Caloric Intake Estimation From Pre Meal Videos And Post Meal Plate Waste

Title is the title of a research paper by Vladimir Kulyukin and Heidi Wengreen

Daft Punk - *Get Lucky*

Alastair Crowley and Rose Edith Crowley / Aiwass - *The Book of the Law*

the only reason i was abducted by aliens in kathmandu in 1994 was that in 1994 i went to kathmandu to be abducted by aliens

Title is from Grant Morrison's 2000 Disinfo.Con lecture

Paul the Apostle - *Second Epistle*

A CHEMTRAIL IN CURVED AIR

Title is a reference to Terry Riley's *A Rainbow in Curved Air*

No Songs

CRASS - *Big A, Little A*

Anna Mendelssohn - *'basalt.'*

Human Fruit Machine

Maria Callas - *'You are born an artist or you are not. And you stay an artist, dear, even if your voice is less of a fireworks.'*